How to Support Your
the Stress of Revis

A Positive and Pra(

by Bernadette Jones

This guide is intended to help parents remain positive and keep a sense of perspective while nurturing and guiding their teenagers through the revision process and exam months. It offers advice and support to parents who are trying to help their teenagers feel confident and good about themselves and their progress. It also aims to empower the students themselves, helping them recognise that they need to take ownership of their studies and adopt a proactive approach to learning.

Edited by Sue Nicholson

Contents

Part 1: Introduction

The premise underpinning this guide is simple. As parents, we love our children and want the best for them in every aspect of their lives. We are increasingly aware of the importance of exam results yet we are also concerned about the potential impact that exam stress can have on both the individual student and the family as a whole. As a consequence, the months leading up to any type of school or university exam - whether mocks or “real” - are of particular concern.

The key goal during exam time is therefore to either completely avoid or, at the very least, minimise stress. Stress can potentially prevent a teenager achieving his or her full potential and even more importantly can impact negatively on that teenager’s health.

Despite this, the desire for success in the form of high grades and levels can prevent many teenagers from recognising stress as a real problem. Others may be more aware of stress as an issue but still feel reluctant to ask for help. Many teenagers may instead continue to push ahead in pursuit of exam results which they believe should be achieved in the same time frame as their peers.

Parents can also have their judgement clouded by the pressure of results. Thus, unlike in many other parenting scenarios, they may not know how or when to intervene. For example, if a parent saw their teenager dangling from a dangerous cliff edge they would respond to their cries for help. A parent would pull their teenager back from danger without hesitation. In this scenario parents would immediately intervene to prevent a potential tragedy. Exam stress is much more complex and often something that both parents and teenagers simply hope will go away. Thus, direct action is not always taken.

As a teacher I have witnessed first-hand a marked increase in mental and emotional health issues amongst teenagers. Many are undoubtedly a direct result of exam pressure. I believe it is essential that parents are provided with clear guidance to help their teenagers adopt healthy attitudes towards exams. The approach of this guide is therefore both positive and practical and aims to avoid unhelpful, negative thinking whenever possible.

While I recognise that to some parents this may sound too good to be true, years of teaching experience have led me to believe that a dramatic reduction in stress at this crucial time is achievable and worth investing time and effort in. I have no doubt there are many things both parents and teenagers can do to actively minimise stress while achieving the best results possible for the individual concerned.

The pressure experienced during the exam months is different for everyone, so this guide should be dipped into and adapted to suit each teenager and family. Teenagers are individuals who want (and are capable of) different things. Each will mature personally and academically in different ways at different times, so the ultimate goal is to give each teenager his or her best chance of achieving success by offering tailored support to minimise stress. And it is parents, in communication with teachers, who are in the best position to recognise their own teenager's specific signs of stress and offer that support.

The value of an education

As adults, we know that education matters and has always mattered. It is possibly the biggest legacy we can leave our children as it provides them with the first step towards true independence and a means with which to secure their futures. We also recognise that education is a door-opener, providing all kinds of opportunities—not just in terms of increased employment opportunities but also in terms of gaining a broader knowledge and understanding of the world, a means by which our children can develop social skills and a strong work ethic.

The educational process should hopefully be a liberating experience—and most people find that qualifications are a positive addition rather than a weight to carry through life! Regardless of whether students claim that they do not care whether or not they pass or fail their exams, or reason that even if they pass they may never use the qualifications they obtain, most will usually accept the fact that qualifications are never a burden—especially if the potential rewards of being qualified are explained to them in terms they can relate to, such as the potential of higher earnings and the chance of securing employment that they will enjoy.

The right approach

It is because our children are individuals that the right approach or combination of approaches can make all the difference. It is often the way that we present information and ideas to our teenagers which determines whether or not they give our suggestions reasonable consideration. It is vital therefore that we address the ways in which each individual student learns and progresses in order to approach exams from the best perspective.

Why us?

And remember: you are not alone. Exam stress of one sort or another is likely to occur in every

household with a teenager, so it will not just be your family in meltdown! Most families will be battling with similar issues, even though the actual experience of stress and a teenager's reactions to that stress will be unique to each individual and household. So no matter how much it feels as though you are the only family struggling at exam time, you can be pretty certain that everyone else is experiencing their own version of exam stress and overload.

The plan

I trust that this guide will go some way towards addressing the issues that arise in many homes at exam time, empowering both parents and students to maximise achievement while minimising stress. When we are given advice we can sometimes dismiss it as obvious, as common sense. Unfortunately when it comes to our teenagers and their exams, 'sense` is not always 'common`. Sense can become clouded by fear, worry, aspirations and even comparisons. Sense therefore is something we may believe we follow but can actually be something we really need reminding of.

The next two sections of the guide explain the concepts behind the roles of both parents and students. The last sections deal specifically with practical approaches through which these roles can be fulfilled.

It is important to stress that the specific type of exam being taken is irrelevant. The focus is on reducing stress for the individual teenager and so this guide is transferable across education systems. Please also note that all names in Case Studies have been changed.

Part 2: Role of the parent in managing stress and keeping a sense of perspective

The key role of parents during the exam months is to encourage their teenagers to aim as high as possible while offering the support needed for them to do so. This requires parents to actively demonstrate ways of reducing stress. While this role sounds (and is) substantial, it is also achievable when parents keep a sense of perspective and think positively. Undoubtedly there will be times when it proves difficult for parents to maintain such a strong position with consistency, but when parents work at imparting positivity as much as they can, this attitude does eventually impact on a teenager's own attitude and approach to learning. In other words, parents should aim to lead by example, modelling positive and healthy behaviours. As part of this approach, parents also need to become active listeners, as the process of advising and directing teenagers can only be improved if there is an awareness and understanding of how the teenagers themselves think and feel.

A further factor to consider as part of the parent's role is the way in which parents perceive themselves. Many parents begin to blame themselves when things are not going well for their children, forgetting how much well-meaning effort and support they have given and continue to give. It is common for parents to act as though they are invincible, attempting to take the strain of the whole household through years of exam cycles. In addition to existing workloads and countless other pressures, this can, for many parents, be simply too much stress to withstand. It can also be counterproductive: if parents neglect themselves, they may end up not being able to provide the support and guidance their children need when they really do need it. And let's be honest, the last thing any parent wants is to be incapable of helping their children when it really matters.

This section of the guide, therefore, aims to provide a reminder of a parent's key roles at exam time.

Key parent role 1: Keeping a sense of perspective and being realistic

Recognising the enemy

Stress is a broad term that covers a wide range of experiences and responses. It can be either student-led or parent-led. As part of keeping perspective, parents need to be aware that regardless of the cause of stress, there is a significant difference between the type of stress driven by a determined desire to achieve and the type of stress driven by a fear of failure and of letting people down. And while the former, potentially positive type of stress can often be readily channelled into a focused programme of exam preparation, the second type of negative and disempowering stress can completely impair a student's ability to take control of his or her own learning, revision and progress. It is therefore essential that parents keep a watchful eye on their teenagers and the type of stress that they are experiencing.

Seeing the bigger picture

A lack of perspective can cause immense stress for both teenagers and parents so it is essential that parents do not lose sight of the bigger picture during exam time. Although exams and the resulting qualifications are hugely significant and, as stated earlier, a key to a potentially bright future we all know that exams are not and never will be, as important as the young people taking them. Therefore a vital aspect of obtaining an education should be that every student is allowed to grow in confidence and encouraged to feel good about themselves and their personal achievements whatever they may be. Consequently, we should not allow the examination system to act as a mechanism that achieves the opposite. In other words, parents need to work towards ensuring that the process of gaining qualifications does not make their teenager feel their specific achievements are inadequate in some way. All progress should be celebrated, regardless of whether it is made slowly or within a different time frame to other students. Ultimately, exams can be retaken and it is never too late to get an education.

Being aware of external factors

In an ideal world, all children would make the best use of their time in school. Unfortunately, this is not always possible. Even the most seemingly dedicated or high-achieving student can stumble or fall victim to circumstance. Any external event, from splitting up with a boyfriend or girlfriend to illness, a poor relationship with a teacher or generally feeling unsupported, can prevent a student from concentrating and achieving his or her best. Witnessing any child crumble under the pressure of external factors is difficult for most parents but it is a heart-breaking experience when it is your own child suffering in this way.

As a consequence of not being able to control everything that happens in our children's lives, the time period directly before and during the exam period can be extremely stressful for both the student taking exams and for their parents and family. And while a degree of stress is an unavoidable part of the exam process, it can, if left unchecked, result in a vicious cycle in which stress can thrive and grow even more. Parents therefore need to keep the exam months in perspective and strive to communicate to their children that life can be unpredictable and that exams are just one component of a much bigger picture.

Reducing parental pressure

When parents demonstrate or communicate a lack of perspective to their teenagers, it may unintentionally result in additional pressure. In fact, regardless of how well-meaning, it can sometimes do more harm than good.

I often encounter students who feel alarmingly worried about letting their parents (or themselves) down, particularly when they feel that the expectations placed on them are too high. Even when a student is perfectly capable of success, he or she will often falter in these circumstances.

Some students experiencing this type of pressure become overwhelmed and freeze, unable to study and revise effectively. Vast amounts of time are then wasted while a student frets about his or her future results and the potential consequences. This is, quite simply, a waste of valuable time that could be spent much more productively on exam preparation.

Students can find such cycles of stress and low productivity extremely difficult to break and need clear guidance when attempting to move forward. The most effective approach in these cases is often best when practical. For example, I routinely find it necessary to sit down with students and help them produce a realistic and achievable timetable (see section on practical approaches). This type of hands-on approach works because it can instantly stop students projecting and magnifying their worries, allowing them instead to focus on the moment in hand.

<u>Case Study: Clare, a Year 13 student</u>

Clare reached a point in February of her final year where she was hardly taking care of herself in terms of eating and sleeping. She had transformed over a few months from a bright and alert student to a visibly pale and weary one. She exhibited all the key signs of stress. Her attendance had become sporadic yet she was not necessarily avoiding her teachers. Instead, she was apologising for her absences to subject teachers, explaining they were a result of the pressures she was under in other subject areas. She could often be found working away in the school building but in the wrong room at the wrong time. She had entered a process of academic juggling in which she attempted to keep one step ahead of her teachers by telling the same excuses and stories in a cycle.

Cycles like this are often resolved when teachers discuss the specific student or, in the case of Clare, when a teacher asks the student directly what is going on, making time for a chat rather than accepting the customary response of "I`m fine." In my experience, when a student is experiencing serious stress, a few kind words when they are least expecting it can result in a full admission that they are not coping, often with a flood of tears. In Clare's case, she had simply become so overwhelmed with the sheer volume of work she had to complete that any attempt to begin revision was superficial and unproductive. As a result, she kept falling further behind, missing more and more lessons to catch up and exacerbating the problem still further.

After many conversations with Clare, it became clear that she needed to go back to basics, so we worked together on a realistic and achievable timetable, which included times to rest and eat. We even went so far as to discuss her diet and plan meals, as it became clear that she was not eating adequately or frequently enough to have any chance of completing her workload. Although Clare's mother was extremely supportive, cooking her daughter healthy meals and giving her the freedom to work in her own way, she was completely unaware of just how little sleep Clare was getting, and that Clare wasn't eating the food provided, instead going without or snacking on chocolate. Her mother had also mistakenly believed that the amount of time Clare spent locked in her room was a measure of productivity.

Creating a clear plan allowed Clare to move forward. It provided her with a structure to follow, immediately taking some of the pressure out of the equation. Removing the worry that she wouldn't fit everything in meant she began sleeping properly again and felt she had time to stop and eat. Clare took control of her study patterns and has reported back that she has continued to use planning as a major component of her learning at the university she now attends.

With adult guidance, a student can learn to trust and follow a plan. He or she can often gain some much-needed peace of mind and stop spending all his or her time worrying about when to do something or about forgetting to do something. Everything is recorded in the plan and every entry has a real period of time allocated to it. The workload can then be approached from a realistic perspective and becomes achievable.

Being realistic about grades and progress

Another aspect of maintaining a realistic perspective concerns the progress grades awarded to students as they study and prepare for their exams. In today's education system and economic climate with its pressure to succeed and be the best, it is not uncommon for students and parents to have adopted a perspective that values only high grades, rather than one that values all aspects of progression.

Parents need to help their teenagers understand that progression is not just about grades and levels, it is about the experience of trying, of facing challenges and of acquiring knowledge that will help them move forward. Parents also need to accept—and help their teenagers to accept—that it is realistic for grades and levels to go down as well as up at different points during a course. Like adults, teenagers are not robots that can be programmed to perform at a consistent or an ever-increasing level. Grades do typically fluctuate for many students. This isn't necessarily a sign that those students are failing. Instead, it may indicate that they are simply going through the process of learning. Every new topic and every new task brings fresh challenges, so it is unrealistic to expect a student to obtain consistently high grades throughout all tasks and across all subjects.

To give an example, an adult proficient at using iMovie would not expect to be as skilled on their first attempt using completely different software, such as Photoshop. They would, however, expect to learn from their first experience and improve on their next and subsequent attempts, possibly changing tactics to learn the new program more effectively. Changing tactics and learning from previous attempts is evidence of effective learning and this type of non-linear progression is exactly the same for a teenager studying for exams.

Recognising the individual

Quite commonly, parents' loss of perspective derives simply from wanting 'the best' for their children. Despite this, parents should ensure that their approach IS actually the 'best' for their teenager as an individual, rather than one that suits their own wants and needs. It is easy and understandable for parents to assume that they are doing the right thing without considering what is realistic or achievable for the teenager concerned. It is also easy for parents to project their own aspirations and experiences (whether good or bad) onto their children.

For example, many parents have a genuine vision of the career they believe will suit their child. Sometimes this vision has become confused with one the parent has at some point aspired to themselves or is connected to a missed opportunity in their own life. It could be a desire for a child to follow directly in the parent's footsteps, or it may simply spring from the parent's understanding of what will make a good and dependable career. This is all well and good if it coincides with what the teenager actually wants. However, if it doesn't, it may be time for the parents to remind themselves to listen carefully to what their teenager has to say about his or her own future.

Many teenagers will express uncertainty about the path they would like to follow, so it may be necessary for parents to encourage their teenager to think about the things they really enjoy and the type of person they are. It may also be appropriate for parents to think about their understanding of the term "aiming high". For many parents, this concept is directly linked to a small number of careers, such as medicine and law yet in reality there are many different paths and opportunities available. It is advisable therefore to ensure that opinions of what aiming high means are not limited by an outdated understanding of what is on offer and that aiming high doesn't have to be restricted to areas of study and work that we, as parents, consider or believe to have a high status. Of course, aiming high as an approach should always be encouraged but parents must strive to understand the aspirations of each teenager as an individual.

<u>*Case Study: Jay, a Year 13 student*</u>

Jay's parents thought everything should be geared towards getting him into a university that they believed would be more respected in the workplace than the one he had chosen for himself. Jay wanted to gain experience in practical film production and, as a result of being an active film-maker, already had a clear vision of the industry and his possible future within it. Jay's parents were not taking Jay's vision or extensive knowledge into account. They were also struggling with the idea that Jay had a better understanding of the course content, teaching style and how it would fit in with his specific learning preferences than they did. Their perspective was understandable and born completely out of their role as parents. They genuinely believed that they knew best because, as adults, they were more experienced—and in many scenarios they were. Jay eventually convinced his parents that he was making the right decision by contacting potential employers in film production and media-based companies and asking them which of the courses they would prefer graduate employees to have studied. All the employers Jay contacted said that they could see more relevance to the industry in the course offered by the university Jay had chosen for himself. In fact, one potential employer said they actively recruited students who had taken this particular course because of the relevance of their skills and knowledge. Luckily for Jay, this was enough to get his parents on board and support his decision (and, I am pleased to report, Jay is now doing really well in his chosen area).

The lesson from Jay's case study is that parents need to be aware that their knowledge isn't always up to date—particularly concerning jobs and areas of work that may not have been commonplace or even existed when they were students. Courses and job opportunities are ever-evolving and should not be dismissed out of hand, simply because we, as parents, do not know much about them. In the future, today's teenagers may be competing for jobs that do not yet exist. To put this into context, think about how many areas of work have developed or changed in terms of the skills now required. When many of us were teenagers, we did not have any knowledge of the potential of the internet—or even know that it was a possibility. We could not conceive of the concept of mobile phones, let alone convergence. Many new jobs have emerged from these developments and many old jobs have disappeared, or have, at least, changed significantly. For example, a mechanic now needs to be computer literate, a gas engineer uses a diagnostic laptop, and surgeons can now operate via video links and robotics.

Moving on

When exams do not go to plan, the focus should always be on the next step. Parents help their children immensely if they can use a situation and specific experience (such as their teenager not achieving the necessary results), as an opportunity to reflect and progress. At times of a setback, it is worth reminding ourselves how we might feel if we were told that we were not doing well enough in a work situation, or falling short in our roles as parents or friends. There may be a lucky few of us who can easily turn disapproval or criticism into a keen desire to improve. However, for most of us, this is a difficult and lengthy process and criticism may even debilitate us for a while. The question parents should ask themselves is whether they really want this to happen to their teenagers during the exam months or when the results come through. Consequently it is important that when things do not go to plan parents choose their words, actions and the timing of their communications with care.

It is preferable in these circumstances to use positive language and to encourage clear focus as far as possible, reminding our teenagers that improvement is always achievable, that there are always alternative approaches to try, and that the courses they wanted to take haven't gone anywhere. It may be that they just need to wait a little longer before they can embark upon their preferred path. It is also worth reminding them that they may even enjoy a course more when their study skills have been further developed after an extra year of reflection and practice. I have seen many students complete a one-year BTEC course after their GCSE's before going on to take A levels—meaning, in effect, three years in the sixth form. Often, these students really benefit from the extra year's study and leave school better prepared than they would have been to tackle either further study or the world of work.

In my experience, many students who have to delay the next level of study do initially experience feelings of disappointment. That is understandable and perfectly natural. However, most express at a later date that they ended up making a more suitable choice, or that it was worth the extra year of study to get a place on the course they really wanted rather than settling for something they could get at the time. It is worth remembering that one of the main reasons for dropping out of university is choosing the wrong course, so it can pay to be patient.

When parents are negative or lose perspective, such as when they communicate tragedy or disappointment if their teenager underachieves, it can easily result in the young person giving up altogether. If a student does not have the confidence to experience failure or is unable to cope with the thought that they are letting their parents down, it is less likely that they will commit to further study or fulfil their true potential. They may even lose faith in themselves. I'm sure many adults have experienced a fear of failure or embarrassment when their work has not been as good as it could have been. Our children feel just as deflated as we do when these experiences happen to them. We therefore need to encourage young people to see failure or underachievement as a temporary obstacle that can be overcome, not as an immovable feature in their lives.

Striking a balance

Of course, parents want their children to achieve their full potential and most will seek to provide every opportunity to facilitate this process. While this is commendable, it can sometimes lead parents to lose sight of the impact and pressure that their ambitions can place upon their teenagers, as well as on themselves. In order to address this problem, parents need to strike a firm balance between realism and ambition. While ambition is to be applauded, a dose of reality can be invaluable, too. It isn't useful, for example, to avoid telling a student who has been predicted C's that they might not secure a place on a course asking for A's. What IS useful is to support them in their pursuit of A's while helping them look at other options in case they do not make the required grades and an alternative route is needed.

Equally, we must remember that while it is important to be honest with students about their progress and realistic about their ambitions and grades, we do not want the reality of their current situation (that is, obtaining C's when A's are required for a particular course) to scare them off or stop them trying. Instead, we want them to recognise that hard work pays off and that the effort they put in now will give them a much greater chance of achieving their ambitions. Even If they do not grasp this concept at once, they will later, for there are always more opportunities if a student adopts the right mind-set.

To convince students of the necessity of hard work, it is sometimes useful to use an analogy they can understand—such as not getting chosen for a team and having to work their way in through practice and effort. Some students can relate to the importance and potential of hard work by thinking about their peers. They all know students who they consider bright but underachieving, describing them as “not being bothered” or “not interested”. They are also familiar with students who they consider intelligent because they achieve consistently good grades. If you encourage teenagers to analyse these different types of student further, most recognise that the students who achieve the best results are the ones who work hard, regardless of how bright others believe them to be. They also start to see that while some students are wasting time, the quiet hard workers are often slowly progressing, at first undetected by their peers (until the grades or levels are handed out). When talking to their teenagers, it is often useful for parents to utilise their teenager’s experience of school to emphasise the value of hard work. Teenagers have been attending school for several years and they know how learning and achieving works. Sometimes, they just need what they already know spelling out for them.

Case Study: Kayla, a Year 11 student

Kayla was an intelligent student who had a tendency to chat or daydream in most of her lessons—a habit that had been discussed at length at parents’ evenings and in correspondence between school and home. Kayla was part of a larger group of girls who, on the surface, appeared more focused on their social lives and current gossip than their work. However, it was interesting to see that when challenged by a teacher, most of the group settled down relatively quickly and returned to task. All, that is, except Kayla, who always felt the need to have the last word and push the situation a little further than everyone else. So while the other girls got back to work, Kayla tried to carry on the joke, with her friends politely humouring her. Consequently, Kayla struggled to finish her work, underachieved and had the reputation among her peers of being the fun one who didn't care. This reputation had come to mean a lot to Kayla, who used it as a source of self-esteem.

When speaking to Kayla and her parents about this cycle, I pointed out that all of Kayla's friends were progressing and doing well. I told her that her friends were handing in their work, even if she didn't actually see them do so. I also reminded her that they were simply doing what they needed to ensure that they got to their chosen next level of study and that none of them were going to jeopardise their own success to keep Kayla company. Finally, I told Kayla that when I asked her friend Sam to stop encouraging her inappropriate behaviour in class by not talking to her, Sam told me Kayla was bright and didn`t need to work as hard as she did. Kayla admitted that she knew that her friends were working and that she wasn't. When asked why she was opting out of her *own learning, Kayla told me that she hadn't thought of it as opting out because, as Sam said, she was quite bright and usually did fine. She also said that she hadn't really thought about their different work levels in terms of long-term consequences such as Higher Education or employment. Kayla became upset at this point but admitted that she didn't want to be the one left behind at the end of Year 11. As a result, she agreed that it would be a good idea for her to be moved to sit elsewhere so she could work without distraction and without distracting others.*

In Kayla's case, she simply needed a reality check. Sometimes, this acknowledgment of reality applies to adults, too. Some parents, for example, need to be realistic in their expectations regarding their teenager's approach to study and their ambitions. We know that even though our teenager may be sitting ten GCSE's and it would be nice to pass them all, in reality he or she may need only five or six to reach the next level, so it isn't necessarily the best option for every young person to resit everything (with the exception of the commonly required English and Maths GCSE's). In other words, it is fine to move on and concentrate on the next level, as in most scenarios it is the next level that counts. Regardless of whether that level is further academic or vocational qualifications, it is likely that experience and the most recent set of qualifications will be the topic of relevance when applying for a course or job. To use an analogy, if you were running in a race and you hit a hurdle you would not run back to take it again if you were already further down the track. The missed hurdle is behind you and does not prevent you from reaching the finishing line. It is in the past and you need to focus on the next hurdle, in the future. Not going back to re-take an exam doesn't necessarily mean a student hasn't learned from the experience of failing or getting a lower than expected grade. It just means that it is probably not necessary to take that particular exam again. In other words, it is important we do not pile pressure on our teenagers by requiring them to resit exams for the wrong or unnecessary reasons.

Case Study: Josh, a Year 13 student

Josh asked me whether he should re-sit an AS exam from Y12 in order to attempt to secure an A at A level. I did not need to answer his question as he quickly answered it himself. During our conversation, he explained that the course he wanted to study did not require an A* and that out of his five university choices, the one that was asking for the highest grades wasn't really the one that he wanted to go to or which offered the course that he most wanted to study. He then reasoned for himself that a resit* *wasn't necessary and he would be better off putting his energy into his current year's work. He finally wondered aloud why he had thought he needed an A* in the first place, stating that it might have been because so many people he knew kept talking about the importance of achieving one that he thought should, too.*

This case study provides a really good example of lost perspective. This particular student was listening to others instead of concentrating on himself and his own needs. In reality, his ambition did not require him to go back and re-take a hurdle.

Josh's story does not suggest that we shouldn't encourage our young people to aim high. I always completely support and advocate stretching and challenging students to achieve their utmost. It is just a reminder that while exams are important and have consequences, the welfare and ambition of the student must always come first. If a failed GCSE is not going to impact on a student's progression to the next level, then there is no reason to pile on pressure with a re-take. If the GCSE is important, however, the exam can obviously be re-taken and it may be that the achievement we crave so badly for our offspring is simply a little further down the road.

Interestingly, it can also be problematic for parents if they have a teenager who becomes obsessed with achieving high grades or one who spends every moment revising. While these students present very different types of worry to the struggling student, they are worries never the less.

Case Study: Zoe, a Year 11 Student

Zoe had become a workaholic, even though from a teaching perspective, she was simply a thorough and diligent model student. After speaking to Zoe and her parents, it became clear they were all concerned that she had become far too anxious about her progress and exam results. Zoe's main problem was that she was spending countless hours revising and then, instead of acknowledging the huge amount of work she had completed, kept focusing on the few aspects she believed she had not covered adequately. This approach was impacting upon her dramatically. She was panicking in exams and freezing for short but key periods of time. I tried to explain to Zoe that she needed to stop berating herself for inadequate preparation, when she had blatantly invested a great deal of time in her study and revision. What Zoe needed was an organised plan, to make sure she covered the essential blocks of revision for each subject and not spend more time than necessary on just one part. Working without a plan meant that Zoe had not been allocating her time effectively and was over-preparing for some parts of a course. While her work ethic was admirable, she needed to be reminded that exams are a stepping stone in order to secure a place at the next level of study. The best way of ensuring that she not only made the leap but did so to the best of her ability was to cover all areas of each course adequately and in proportion to the mark scheme.

Other students are a concern because they are either in denial regarding their own abilities or are simply too frightened of what they consider failure to attempt the tasks presented to them. They have often become focused on high grades and have bought into the culture of seeing anything below the highest levels as underachievement. They consequently do not progress as they are not willing to go through the process of accepting setbacks and moving on from them as a means of progression.

Case Study: Jorge, a Year 11 student

Jorge was frightened of failure and had, to a certain extent, lost sight of reality. He had become fixated on achieving high grades but had forgotten that he needed to be able to achieve them independently.

In other words, he was constantly looking for a quick fix. Instead of investing time in practising and developing his own skills and knowledge, he had fallen into the trap of copying and pasting chunks of information into his notes that he didn't fully understand, or even copying the work of others and attempting to claim it as his own. This was a huge worry as a lot of his work had been superficial and quite frankly a waste of time. The real problem manifested itself in timed and unseen work as he had not been able to pre-prepare or memorise material and had therefore not been able to attempt the tasks. In conversation, Jorge had fallen into the habit of presenting himself as someone who wasn't confident in exams, even though this had never been properly put to the test as he had avoided having a genuine go at any. Although this was a delicate issue to deal with, there was no substitute for addressing the truth and that was essentially what had to happen. Jorge was extremely upset when confronted about his practice of copying work from the internet or from others—and even more upset when he had to face the fact that he was avoiding the reality of his situation by avoiding taking part in timed tests. He told me that he felt that everyone he knew seemed to be able to achieve well in exams and he was worried that he was not as good and so had started to take work he thought was better from elsewhere. He had now become frightened of failing and didn't know how to break the cycle. I pointed out that he had to run his own race and that comparison with others was not helping him. I reminded him that while he was comparing, others were working and making progress. This was a hard lesson for Jorge to learn but ultimately being told the truth was the best thing for him as he became willing to have a go and started to move forward. His confidence increased and, in the future, the grades and levels he achieves will be his own. He will also be much better equipped to deal with new courses of study.

Sometimes a fear of failure can lead some teenagers to hide from reality. For example, some teenagers who are struggling with heavy workloads have a tendency to hide from their worries rather than face up to them. The amount of stress this places upon them can be quite alarming as they end up spending days on end avoiding teachers and live in constant dread of a phone call home from school to their parents. To a worried teenager a phone call which will expose what they perceive as their failure, is immensely embarrassing as the cycle of 'hiding' often started from either a fear of letting people down or from an inability to admit that they are not coping. These situations are particularly upsetting as they could often have been avoided by simply keeping the lines of communication between the student and their parents open. Consequently, it is vital that when a student does tell a parent that they are not coping that the parent concerned really listens to that student and tries to understand how they feel without judging. Often solutions that seem obvious to parents are not obvious to their children. What may seem like a minor issue to an adult can feel like an insurmountable problem to a teenager.

Accepting a different point of view

Parents are older, more experienced and of a different generation to the teenagers they are guiding. Consequently, they need to recognise that teenagers are not necessarily going to share their point of view or believe that they are right without question. This attitude is not necessarily a deliberate undermining of authority. It is simply a more youthful take on a particular situation. Rather than assuming that a teenager will automatically agree with our reasons for wanting them to revise, it is our role to explain the value of exams and qualifications, while listening to what the teenagers themselves have to say.

Sometimes, the experience of a parent feels irrelevant to a young person, as the system they are in and the attitudes they come up against have changed. In this scenario, even though parents may expect recognition of their experiences, they may not receive automatic understanding. It is often the case that parents need to think carefully about how they communicate their personal experiences so that their teenager can understand and benefit from their knowledge.

Fostering partnerships

Parents cannot take sole responsibility for everyone during the exam months. There are just too many roles to be fulfilled. Parents need to look after themselves and possibly other children, too, and that is why partnerships (between home and school as well as between parents and children) should be encouraged.

In my experience, there are occasions when some parents view school and teachers as the enemy—a view that is not helpful for either the parent or teenager concerned. Teachers want their students to succeed, and it is strong partnerships between parents and teachers that will help students achieve that success. It is particularly beneficial for students if parents encourage them to have an open and honest dialogue with their teachers about their work and progress. It is also helpful if parents recognise that sometimes their teenager may not appear to get on with a particular teacher and may even go through a phase of complaining about that teacher, in the same way that an adult might complain about their boss or a colleague. This does not automatically mean that the teacher is at fault or that the teenager seriously dislikes the teacher. It may simply be a case of a student “offloading”. In fact, it is worth remembering that while teenagers occasionally express dissatisfaction with a teacher to their parents, they may also express dissatisfaction with their parents to their teacher—perhaps in terms of their struggle to meet high expectations, or their feelings that their parents do not fully understand the pressure they are under. This, of course, does not mean the parent is at fault or that the teenager seriously dislikes them. It is again simply a case of the student “offloading” under pressure.

Understandably, in such a scenario parents would be keen to defend themselves and their actions. Similarly, teachers would be keen to justify and explain their actions in terms of their role—one that is both significant and complex, involving dealing with students as individuals as well as part of a class. The teacher’s role and the student’s relationships with their teachers are crucial, so ideally parents and teachers need to support each other as much as they can. Teachers want all their students to succeed, and they invest a great deal of time into helping them do so. Obviously teachers do not have the same emotional attachment to their students as the students’ parents, but this is a good thing. Parents of teenagers need the help and support of adults with an unclouded and realistic judgement to provide balance. And with a positive input from everyone concerned, each teenager will have the best chance of success.

Summary

Keeping a sense of perspective and being realistic are essentially grounded in common sense. Avoid letting revision and exam periods become disproportionate to the rest of your teenager's and family's lives and remember: No amount of achievement is worth putting anyone's health at risk.

Key parent role 2: Being supportive and thinking positively

Communicating the positives

One specific role of the parent during stressful exam cycles is to intercept stressful messages that may have unwittingly lost touch with reality. A classic example of this is when a teenager has somehow absorbed the notion that failing an exam or underachieving in any capacity is the end of the world. This type of misconception can be worrying for a parent as ultimately the unrealistic perspective upon which it is founded may be detrimental to any student achieving his or her full potential. Young people are less likely to perform well if they are worrying prematurely about failure.

Parents, therefore, need to focus on communicating positive and optimistic messages in order to combat any unhelpful thought processes—which are very easy to adopt when under pressure. It is alarmingly easy for a teenager to believe that the exams they are undertaking are everything and that failing or underachieving in any of those exams is a disaster. We need to remember that realistically there are many reasons and situations that may lead to a student underachieving and having to rethink options. There are many reasons, too, which mean individuals take longer than intended to reach their goals. Sometimes, students have simply chosen the wrong courses, ones to which they are not suited. Others may have decided to take gap years at different points in their education, while others may simply have personal circumstances or experiences that prevent them from achieving their potential at a particular time. So if a young person ends up having to re-sit exams or having to change their initial direction, it is definitely not the end of the world. In fact, sometimes it is the beginning of something better, which may result in greater long-term happiness.

When trying to maintain perspective parents must always look for the positives in every situation, as the opposite approach does not help. This is something that cannot be stressed enough.

During my years as a teacher, I have come across many students who are extremely self-critical and who struggle with any form of criticism, even when it is constructive and well-meant. For some of these students, the communication that failing an exam is the worst thing that could ever happen to them has resulted in patterns of negative thinking which, in a few cases, has been interpreted by the individual concerned as evidence that they as a person have little of value to offer. I always remind these students, who believe that school exam success or failure is the main criteria by which they will be judged in life, that if this were true it suggests that unless we all achieve our full potential between the ages of 16 and 18, we will be stuck as that person forever with no further opportunities or achievements to look forward to. I think everyone would agree this is an unhelpful thought and definitely not an outlook parents would want their children to have. So while we must encourage our teenagers to aim high, we must also be realistic. Ultimately, exams can be re-taken, so there is no reason for teenagers to absorb unnecessary pressure. There is a lot of living and achieving still to be done after the age of 18, so although some people may take longer than they intended to reach their goals, the best message to convey to our teenagers is that a longer route is absolutely fine and just as valid.

Case Study: Safia, a Year 13 student

Safia was a bright student who did not apply herself during her GCSE's and consequently underachieved. She did not believe she was particularly able and did not socialise with peers who encouraged her either actively or by example. Although at the back of her mind she wanted to do well and had ambition, she did not recognise that there was a clear connection between her work ethic and success in achieving that ambition. As a result, Safia had to re-sit her GCSE English examination and, as she did not have the grades necessary to start A levels, had to sign up to a BTEC course that she did not really want to do. Many students in Safia's position lose heart, feeling as though they have been left behind. Safia took the opposite approach. She worked hard and excelled on her BTEC course, achieving a distinction. She also passed her English GCSE and was subsequently allowed to do A levels as she had proved to her teachers that she had dedication. She achieved A's and B's at AS level, then again at A2, and went on to the university of her choice, studying the subjects she initially wanted to pursue. The lesson here is simple.

Safia did not give up. She worked hard and she achieved her goals, despite having to take a longer route to get there.

Playing a supporting role

The most important factor when guiding teenagers through the exam months is to remember that they, as students, have to take the lead roles and we, as parents, are aiming for supporting roles. In other words, exams are about the students, not their parents—after all, we can only play the lead in our own lives!

Teenagers really do need the support of their parents, as the exam months can be genuinely stressful and each will respond to this period of time differently. A parent's knowledge of their own child, in addition to that parent's willingness to listen and support their child is therefore vital.

As parents, we need to remind our teenagers that their education is about what THEY want to do, and not what we as parents want them to do. Teenagers need to choose their own path, and a parent's role is to help them recognise which qualifications are needed to get to the next level. It is helpful, therefore, when parents acknowledge that if a student has their own goals and therefore a vested interest in their studies, it is much more likely that they will succeed.

Even if students are unsure of the specific course or courses that they would like to study, parents need to support them by reminding them of the importance of aiming high whenever possible. In such scenarios, where a student is unsure of his or her direction, it is vital that they keep in mind that when they do eventually decide their future path, a chosen course may still have minimum entry requirements. The aim is therefore to always to do as well as possible in all exams in order to maximise choice. In some ways, this is even more vital when a student is unsure what they want to do, as then they have more chance of being prepared for any eventuality. They do not want to rest on their laurels only to find that when they do make a decision their grades are inadequate.

Supporting teenagers taking control of their own destiny is something really positive that parents can do to help, as the need for independence is only going to increase as a young person goes through school and life. A parent's role will always be important, but as a key support not director. When students genuinely have no idea what they would like to do next, their parents can discuss the options available, but they cannot make up their teenagers minds for them. A parent's role is to encourage their teenager to do their best and to keep their options open. This is one of the most effective ways of minimising stress.

<u>Case Study: Rachel, a Y13 student</u>

Rachel was sure of only one thing, and that was that she did not want to continue with any of the A level subjects she was studying. She felt that she might quite like the idea of doing something practical but outside this she was completely stuck. She consequently had little choice but to focus on her current exams and aim as high as possible in the hope that when she did finally made a decision, she would have obtained the grades she needed. It was important that Rachel understood that while it was not a good idea for her to pursue a degree or career in which she was not interested, she did not want to find herself without a next step when she received her exam results in the summer. While she did not want to continue with any of her current subjects long term, out of the three A levels she was taking, she enjoyed Art the most—and it was practical. After many discussions with her parents and teachers, Rachel decided to apply for a one-year art foundation course. With the help of supportive adults she was able to step back from the need to make a firm, long-term decision - and a direction did emerge. After taking her art foundation, Rachel decided to apply for a degree in making theatre props and set design. She had just needed more time and the encouragement from her parents to make a bridging decision which took away the stress of making the wrong choice.

Another specific scenario that requires parents to continue to offer key support is when their teenager seems reluctant to put in enough effort by themselves. This role can be difficult but is definitely worth the extra support from a parent in the long run. As a teacher, I always remind these students that by simply turning up they have made a commitment to learning and, as they are at least physically present in lessons, they may as well use the time wisely. If they do not, it is simply a waste. If re-sitting an exam does become necessary, then parents should remember that for some students, resits are an important part of the maturing process and a chance for them to become efficient at studying. In cases like this, parents should support their teenagers by helping them recognise that they are still moving forward. As part of this support, it is worth utilising teenagers' own ambitions and aspirations as far as possible, as most young people crave a future that requires some level of education and usually respond well to this approach.

Despite all our best efforts and the existence of strong working partnerships, parents may still struggle to persuade their teenager to focus, or to alleviate all their stress at exam times. This may be attributable to the stage that particular teenager is at, or simply down to the type of person they are. Not everyone can have a teenager who naturally studies. In these scenarios, maintaining a positive relationship with the teenager is vital so that in the future, when that teenager is more ready and willing to accept support, parents will be in a position to help. It is important that parents recognise that a teenager who appears unwilling to work, regardless of the reason, is not evidence that the parent-child relationship has broken down. It is firm evidence that the parent-child relationship is still very much needed.

The next level

When a student makes it to the next level of study, it is essential that parents recognise that this is not just a time to celebrate but also a time to keep a watchful eye on stress levels as for many the transition can be daunting. Some students struggle with the experience of finding themselves at the bottom of a new ladder. Many have recently worked really hard to secure their best possible grades and so feel disheartened when they realise that they are now being measured against new standards. The reality for many is that they are suddenly receiving lower grades or levels. For some, this feels like failure and they worry that they are not going to be able to cope. Parents need to reassure them that they are now studying at a higher and more challenging level. It is not realistic to expect to achieve high scores overnight. A further issue to be aware of is that many students at this stage may have a part time job in addition to an increasing social life. This can be a lot to manage and so parents may need to help their teenager organise their time. With regard to working and volunteering which are both admirable pursuits, parents need to try and help their teenagers strike a balance. For example, agreeing to extra shifts at work if a student is struggling with study may not be advisable. However if a student really feels they need to work due to personal circumstances, they will need all the support and understanding they can get.

Case Study: Elsie, a new Y12 student

Elsie did well in her GCSE's and was pleased with her results. She achieved A's and B's in the subjects she wanted to study for A Level and B's and C's in the rest. This was a fantastic achievement and she entered Y12 excited and looking forward to her new courses. Within the first few weeks Elsie was disheartened, exhausted and tearful. She was finding her school work much harder than it was in Y11 and she did not understand the homework's she had been set. In addition Elsie had just started a part-time job and had agreed to hours without realising the impact it could have upon her studies. She was unwilling to let her new employer down as she was worried that she would appear unreliable. She was also trying to make new friends. Long hours at work in addition to long hours spent on homework, resulted in floods of tears and a belief that she was not good enough to complete her courses. Elsie needed a great deal of support at this stage from her parents and a few very simple measures helped immensely. Elsie's parents were both positive and practical. Firstly they made sure that Elsie had enough sleep and gave her some much needed attention. They then spent time reading through her homework tasks with her to try and help her understand what she needed to do. They also helped her work out how to explain to her new employer in a mature and sensible way that she could not work as many hours as she had previously thought. Elsie's parents helped her organise her time so that she could catch up with school work and they encouraged her to trust her teachers (Elsie had been frightened and embarrassed to show her new teachers her work as she felt it wasn't good enough.) Elsie had just not realised that the leap from Y11 to Y12 would be so substantial and was not prepared. She also felt that she should be able to tackle everything alone. Her parents reduced her stress by making her understand that she was not alone: she had her parents and teachers to support her whenever she needed them.

This was enough to get Elsie back on track. She recognised that she was simply on a new level of learning and at a different point in her life. Struggling was not a sign that she was inadequate. It simply meant that she was at the beginning of a new and challenging journey.

This case study highlights how on-going parental support really benefits a teenager who is finding study and exams stressful. The positive input of a parent can help a teenager develop the next stage of their independence as they ease themselves into a more adult world. A balance between study, work and social life is essential if they are to succeed. Parents can use their vast experience to advise and model ways of achieving this.

Making use of your knowledge

While there are many supportive approaches and strategies beneficial to most young people during the exam months, the most appropriate and effective support will always originate from a parent's special and unique knowledge of their own child—knowledge gained through the actual experience of parenting them. That said, all parents should remember that just as we have many facets to our personalities, so do our teenagers. This means that it is not only the parent's knowledge of a teenager that matters. Some aspects of their personalities will not necessarily be revealed at home, so the knowledge that teachers have of how individual teenagers learn and respond to specific exam situations—whether in lessons, controlled assessments or exams themselves— is also invaluable. We therefore need to make use of the combined knowledge available to tailor support specifically to a student's individual needs.

If parents acknowledge that the process of obtaining an education and qualifications is a different experience for each individual, they will understand that each individual requires different levels of direction and support—that is, some children study and organise themselves more readily and easily than others. In recognition of this individuality, it is probably wise if parents avoid comparing their teenager to other young people as no matter how similar their situations may seem on the surface, there will be enough differences to make comparison futile. We must also remember that the issue of avoiding comparisons is not just about avoiding comparing children with their peers, but also about parents avoiding comparison with other parents.

Encouraging independence

Most parents really do go the extra mile to protect and support their teenagers during exams. However, the remit of being supportive doesn't necessarily translate into doing everything for our children. In fact, a key part of supporting teenagers is encouraging them to develop their independence. If we allow our teenagers to take some control and responsibility for their studies, we will be doing them a great deal of good in the long run. We will be equipping them to succeed, not just in their exams, but in many other areas of life. In effect, we will be teaching them that they are capable of success.

True academic independence requires students to develop ownership and pride in their own work so it is extremely important to find a balance between hand holding and giving them a free rein. For example, it is not always beneficial to leave all students completely to their own devices. Equally, if we want a student to become an independent learner, we do sometimes have to step back so they can experience coping with, and surviving, high-pressured situations.

This is a fundamental reason why it is important to encourage teenagers to start preparing for exams early whenever possible, as extra time will allow them to develop their independence, learn from their mistakes and follow up by achieving their potential.

The difficult lesson for parents is that sometimes underachievement is unavoidable on the route to independence. Many individuals, including parents and teachers, may have experienced underachievement or failure at some point in their education or careers, and most will have survived the experience.

The key message is for parents to be supportive but avoid taking over and doing everything for their teenager. Otherwise, parents may find themselves still heavily involved when their children are studying at university or even starting a new job! Taking over and even completing work on a student's behalf makes both failure and success pointless as in real terms the student will gain little from either.

Modelling positive thinking

As adults we often cite the old adage that how we deal with failure shows the measure of true character. However, despite this, parents understandably struggle to apply or embrace the concept with regard to their own children and may also behave and think negatively when problems arise. As parents, we need to avoid promoting one rule for ourselves and a different one for our children. In other words, we need to model positive thinking.

It is quite common for parents to be understanding and positive when someone else's child has a setback but have a tendency to act out their own disaster movie when their own teenager struggles or does not do as well as they hoped in an exam. Remember that teenagers know their parents and their tendencies just as well as the parents know them and theirs. It is therefore understandable that if a teenager becomes aware of any disproportionate disappointment communicated by their parents towards an achievement, they may feel, at times, equally disappointed in the parent concerned. So not only do parents need to take a deep breath and choose their words (and their facial expressions) wisely, they also need to offer support by actually thinking positively about their teenager's situation. Being supportive means exactly that. It is not an opportunity to be judgemental or to make unfair comparisons; it is a chance to help. And parents need to be aware that non-verbal communication can be just as powerful as words.

Communicating key messages

There is always a chance that your teenager will not want to listen to advice, but this does not mean that you, as parent, should stop communicating positive messages. These can be communicated most successfully first by explaining and then by demonstrating, or modelling, positive behaviour and attitudes. In this way, parents can let their teenagers know that they really do see all their achievements in a positive light, are proud of their progress and genuinely optimistic about their future. It must be noted that communicating key positive messages through explanation and modelling is not a part-time job. Parents need to be consistent and persistent and should try not to deviate from this path. Some teenagers will resist believing positive messages for months on end but if parents continue to model them, most will eventually recognise their worth.

<u>Case Study: Nikita, a Year 12 student</u>

Nikita was disappointed with his exam results at GCSE and did not believe his parents when they said that they were proud of him and thought that he had done well. Nikita had a tendency to panic in exams and consequently felt that he would automatically underachieve in any exam he sat. His parents, however, knowing that he panicked, genuinely felt he had done well and were extremely proud that he had passed. His parents constantly reassured him that they were happy and impressed with his results; I spoke to Nikita and confirmed the same. This became a regular dialogue between all parties with no change in Nikita's stance until about a year later, when Nikita announced that his GCSE results probably weren't as bad as he had thought and that he now believed his parents' assertion that his results were testament to his commitment and wouldn't stop him achieving at the next level. When asked what had changed his opinion, Nikita said that, on reflection, what his parents had been saying suddenly made sense to him, especially now he was doing well on his AS courses, despite having lower grades than some of his peers. The persistence of Nikita's parents, in addition to the time Nikita needed to absorb the message they were communicating, eventually paid off. When I spoke with Nikita about this again at a later date he said that part of the reason that he wanted to do well was because his parents had always encouraged and supported him yet had never put him under any pressure to do more than he could do. He also said that they were always pleased no matter how he did. Nikita's parents had consistently modelled positive attitudes and behaviours and Nikita eventually recognised their worth and adopted those attitudes for himself.

Taking a step back

If parents recognise that their part in their children's success is in a supporting role only, they should also be able to recognise that this means, on a practical level, taking a step back. Parents need to listen to their teenager's point of view and then explain their own perspective, without suggesting they are always and definitely right. While many may think that this sounds too amicable to be true, I would argue that shouting, screaming and dictating rarely works. It may have a temporary impact but rarely aids a long-term dialogue. It may also be useful in letting off a bit of steam but usually results in everyone feeling sorry for the harsh words inflicted, with at least one person reduced to tears (just as often a parent) and everyone vowing to start again with a more supportive approach.

Taking a step back can sometimes require parents to continue to offer support even when it seems unwanted. Some teenagers may simply not accept the advice or input of a parent. Some may refuse to study or revise in any capacity at all. Others will claim persistently that they know what they are doing when you, the parent, are convinced they do not. Parents should not give up on their teenagers at this point, or withdraw their support. As individuals, we can only control our own role and make sure that it is delivered to the best of our ability. This doesn't mean we will suddenly become saints, never lose our tempers or never feel frustrated with the situation. However, it will hopefully mean that we will actively try to maintain a sense of perspective in that we will act out our role as the adult and parent, even though this can mean sometimes having to make difficult decisions when our children can't, wont or don't know how to do so for themselves.

Sometimes, as parents, we struggle to take a step back and allow our teenagers to experience failure. Some parents go so far as to complete work on behalf of their child in order to ensure they succeed. This isn't the best approach, even if it achieves a temporary result. Parents simply need to focus on their teenagers as learners and let them learn in the way that is best for them. If this involves a few knocks along the way, then ultimately the teenagers will be stronger and more independent as a result of the experience.

Case Study: Kat, a Year 12 student

Kat had started to submit work that was not her own. It transpired that her work was being completed mainly by a parent so, understandably, when Kat had to complete class work or take an exam, there was a huge discrepancy in the levels achieved. When challenged about this, Kat was embarrassed and reluctant to speak. The lesson here is that Kat did not benefit from this experience. If anything, it had a negative impact on her, as even though the parent concerned really did mean well, the message communicated to Kat was that her own work was not good enough. In the future, Kat's feeling of failure will only get worse if she does not achieve as well as she would like in her exams. A much healthier approach would be for Kat's parent to work with Kat not for her. That way she would learn from the experience and have an opportunity to value her own development. While parents taking an interest and supporting their teenagers is always welcomed, parents must avoid doing all the work for a student. In Kat's case, it provided a quick fix but in the long run it caused a crisis of confidence.

Summary

The role of being supportive is about stopping and thinking whether your words and actions will actually benefit your teenager in any way. It is about taking a step back and recognising that your teenager is a different person to you and that you cannot direct their every move. Instead, you have to listen, advise and help them execute the plan for their life that THEY have decided upon. Of course, parents need to remain assertive regarding key parenting decisions about behaviour and attitudes towards family rules, health and safety. Parental assertiveness is less helpful regarding how their teenager learns, or their future career path.

Key parent role 3: Identifying and dealing with stress

Parents know their own children and their children's specific responses to many different situations but they may not have necessarily seen them in a state of exam stress before. The following list includes some possible signs of stress to look out for, all of which commonly appear in students. The list is by no means exhaustive and if you are ever worried about your child's health at exam time, you should seek help through school, the family doctor or perhaps friends and other family members.

Common signs of stress

Common signs of stress may include:

- A loss of appetite.
- Complaining of frequent low level illnesses, such as headaches or stomach pains.
- Feeling tearful.
- Difficulty concentrating.
- Negative thought patterns.
- Seeming irritable.
- Not looking after appearance.

- Missing lessons at school.
- Changes to social habits e.g. going out much more or much less than usual.

Key daily support

If students are going to manage exam stress and perform to the best of their ability, they need to be physically fit and rested. Here, therefore, are ten basic rules to help ensure your teenager is in optimum shape.

Ten Basic Rules:

1. Make sure your teenager is eating a nutritious, balanced diet and drinking enough water.
   Many studies show that inadequate hydration levels seriously impact on concentration and exam performance. It is best to avoid foods high in sugar and fat as they can cause lethargy and make it harder for the body to deal with stress.
2. Make sure your teenager is getting enough good quality, undisturbed sleep.
   Sleep is necessary before learning as it results in the brain being better prepared to take in new information. Getting enough sleep also means that the brain is able to form key memories out of new learning. Sleep is also

essential after learning as during sleep the brain saves and stores that new learning, thereby strengthening memory. A lack of sleep can therefore reduce a student's ability to concentrate and turn new learning into fixed memories, that can be more easily recalled.

3. Ensure that your teenager has an organised and quiet space in which to study.

   Filing and ordering work helps students avoid wasting valuable time looking for the things they need.

4. Encourage your teenager to study in a way that suits them.

   Different teenagers feel comfortable studying in different ways. Some like some quiet music; others prefer silence. Some may hum or even tap a foot against the desk. Try to avoid assuming their style is wrong just because it isn't a method you automatically associate with learning.

5. Switch off mobile phones and computers at bed time.

   Electronic devices are not just a distraction; they can also exaggerate any existing vulnerability, as many young people continue social correspondence via text and social networking sites when they should be asleep. Young people are more susceptible to insecurity at night, so this type of contact can be inappropriate on many levels. For example, if your teenager is experiencing any worries or concerns or is involved in any conflicts, communication at night time is not going to help improve their sleep or aid their studies.

6. Allow your teenager to live a little.

   Avoid constant talk about exams and consequences of not doing well. Teenagers need time away from the pressure of exams. Try to avoid working exams and progress into every conversation. Parents often talk about exams to alleviate their own concerns. This is completely understandable but not necessarily helpful.

7. Stay calm to avoid a meltdown.

   Tempers are easily fraught at exam time. I know this is easier said than done, but try counting to 10 ten before entering into a potentially heated debate with a stressed or difficult teenager. Most parents are familiar with how much worse situations can become when tempers get out of control.

8. Try not to isolate your teenager from the rest of family.

   During exam time, we often focus so intensely on the student sitting exams that parents can both neglect other members of the family and keep the exam student alienated. It is easy to inadvertently run a household where everyone is living completely separate lives. The support and company of siblings is important for the exam student, too.

9. Listen to your teenager.
   The simple act of listening works wonders for any relationship. When parents listen to their teenager, the teenager concerned instantly feels valued and is more likely to listen in return.
10. Encourage your teenager to exercise.
   Regular exercise will reduce the chance of your teenager becoming ill as it boosts the immune system. It will also help your teenager maintain a healthy weight and increase energy levels. Physical activity improves mood, reduces stress and allows people to gain a sense of perspective. Exercise will improve a teenager's ability to concentrate and study.

Key messages to communicate

Good communication with your teenager often requires a great deal of negotiation, requiring a parent both to ask their teenager questions and to listen to the answers—in the same way that any two adults would try to communicate. Here are some worthwhile messages to communicate, which focus on the positives in any situation.

- It is never too late to improve.
- All progress is worthwhile.
- Coursework, controlled assessments and exam practice do matter.
- Organising your work, revising and practising really helps.
- Taking control of your own study leads to independence and long-term success.
- If a method isn't working, change it and try something else.
- Achievement in exams results in opportunities, so exams are worth pursuing.

Ten tips for keeping sane

In order for the whole family to survive the exam months parents need to encourage and adopt sensible approaches and routines.

1. Remember that the teenager taking exams is only one person in the whole family. The happiness of the family as a unit matters to everyone in that unit. There is no point in focusing on one child at the expense of another. Children who are not doing exams may have other issues just as important. In addition, siblings can develop their own

symptoms of stress when they are worried about changes they have observed in either the person taking exams or in a parent at exam time.

2. Use exam time as a chance for the whole family to adopt positive practices. The exam months can be the perfect time for everyone to adopt healthy routines. All family members will benefit from good quality sleep, a balanced diet and time to relax.

3. Avoid putting your lives on hold. If you have more than one child, you could write off years in a long cycle of exam stress. Parents can sometimes be in danger of getting stuck in an exam rut, where all they do is worry about, and pursue, exam results. There is only so much a parent can do to help. As parents, we must remember to spend time investing in other areas of our lives as well.

4. Make sure that you tell your teenager that you genuinely support and love them. It sounds obvious but sometimes during periods of stress parents can forget to tell their teenagers just this. There is no substitute for being told that someone genuinely cares about you—and the exam months are definitely a time when a teenager needs to feel secure.

5. Keep all lines of communication open.
Communicate in any way possible. Never stop speaking to your teenager even if they stop speaking

to you. Also, if your teenager prefers to speak to your partner, a sibling, a teacher, another relative or a family friend, accept this as a positive and a much-needed support. Sometimes speaking to someone who is less emotionally involved is easier for the teenager concerned, and not a deliberate rejection of a parent.

6. Have clear rules and boundaries about behaviour and stick to them. Allowing family rules and boundaries to be broken at exam time is short-sighted and will not help towards achieving a stress-free house. During the exam months, it can be tempting to let things go but the reality is that this is a time when you need consistency and when your teenager needs to know exactly where he or she stands. Bending rules at this time can lead to a teenager taking advantage of new freedoms and doing less worthwhile study, not more.

7. Be the adult and make decisions when necessary. Never forget your role as parent. You make the rules and even though negotiation can be a positive practice, ultimately the health and safety of the whole family is the parent's responsibility, so do not shy away from taking control.

8. Use all practical approaches as examples only. Nothing is set in stone. Everyone approaches study

in his or her own way. It is not a good idea to impose an approach on your teenager. Instead, model examples and let your teenager choose what works for them.

9. Praise achievements but be realistic. It is really healthy and positive to praise achievement, but parents must be careful that they do not fall into the habit of praising as a means of protecting their teenagers from the truth. If teenagers are praised even when they have not done anything worthy of praise, they may develop a false perception of themselves and their capabilities—and this can lead to a great deal of disappointment when the results come in.

10. Give treats not bribes. Small treats can help a teenager through their revision programme, providing a welcome break and an emotional lift at crucial times, when stress levels are rising. Bribes, however, are not part of a healthy work ethic and are, in my view, unnecessary. Parents need to demonstrate that achieving your best is something to be proud of and something to build on as an approach to life.

Summary

Identifying and dealing with stress is about a parent being observant and intervening when necessary. Creating routines and structures that prevent stress from occurring is always a parent's first line of defence. If stress does occur, it is all about moving quickly and decisively. And remember, positive and open communication will always aid these interventions.

Part 3: Role of the student in taking ownership and responsibility

(This section is written specifically for the student in your family. Please encourage your teenager to read it.)

This guide has been written for students like you who are in the middle of, or are about to embark upon revision towards exams. For many this can be a stressful time and so I have provided a few pointers to help you keep exams and revision in perspective.

Be kind to the future you

As a student it is important to recognise that it is in your own interest to achieve your full potential. It is vital to aim high while trying to retain a realistic perspective as it is YOUR future and YOUR future alone that your achievements will really impact upon. As a student, you need to try to take responsibility for your own learning as your teachers and parents will not be there to help you in the exam hall! Remember: You are working hard now to make life easier for the future you.

Be prepared

Most of us would accept that there are very few people who could realistically enter a marathon without undergoing any training and yet still expect to win, so the question is why do some students assume they can turn up to an exam and achieve the highest grades or levels without adequate preparation. It sounds obvious yet many students can specifically attribute previous underachievement to the fact that they did not revise thoroughly, instead opting to 'wing it' on the day. What would you think of an Olympic athlete or a professional footballer who said that they were not going to bother to train but would just take their chances on the day? I am not sure anyone would respect that attitude. So always use any time you have available to prepare for exams. Even the smallest amount of training is better than none (though enough preparation is obviously best of all!).

Understand your parents

As a student you need to remember that your parents are concerned about you, so often the words and behaviours they use, which may appear to you as nagging or overreacting, are simply a result of their emotional involvement in your progress. Remember they have probably spent your whole life worrying about you and it is difficult for them to stop now. Consequently, it is probably a good idea to cut your parents some slack and speak to them about what is going on with your studies at this crucial time.

Keep communicating

As a student you need to try your best to communicate how you are feeling. This isn't always easy, particularly if adults do not appear to be listening, but you must try. A good technique is to ask for a parent or teacher to listen without interruption so you have room to explain yourself fully. Sometimes we can all say things in a confused or clumsy way and we need a chance to re-explain what we actually meant to convey. When people interrupt or comment before we can finish, the point or message can be lost or misinterpreted, so do ask for time and patience on the part of your listener.

Take control

It is important that you take control of your own ambition and decide where you are going and how and when you intend to get there. When you show that you are in control of your studies, it is much more likely that your parents will listen. It is often a lack of ownership and work ethic on your part that leads to parents becoming over-involved and consequently adding extra pressure to the situation. It is understandable that your parents will assume that you lack focus and direction if you do not demonstrate otherwise.

Ten top tips for students

As a student you are already aware of the negative impact that exam stress can have if it gets out of control. You are also aware of the importance of passing exams and the joy that it brings. This is why you need to act now and take control of your own learning experience. By using all the support and advice available, you can avoid unnecessary stress and direct your own future.

1. Concentrate only on the things you can change

The past has happened, so there is absolutely no point in dwelling on it and stressing about old work, or work you never did in the first place. New work is the future, so that is where your focus should be. Students who panic are often panicking about the things they think they didn't do.

2. Take ownership of your learning

Become an academic athlete and train for success. The most effective way of avoiding exam stress is to be prepared which means doing everything that you can realistically do. Remember the first step towards being prepared is to organise your space and time. (See section on making a timetable.)

3. Be honest with yourself

You know whether you are working or not, so be honest with yourself about your progress and commitment. You know whether or not you are improving. Lying to yourself about your progress is a waste of time and energy.

4. Stick to the script

Sticking to the script means staying with what you know: do not choose to experiment at exam time. It is amazing how many students write about different texts and materials to the ones they have actually studied in class, or decide to try out a new exam technique on the day of an exam.

5. Attend school

There is no substitute for going to lessons. Many students say they stop going to lessons because they're boring or because they don't feel like they are doing anything worthwhile in them. Trust your teachers and your peers and try not to pick and choose when to take things seriously. There will always be something worthwhile in an activity, even if is only a chance to consolidate learning or ask a question. The simple fact is that the students who attend school do better than those who don't.

6. Listen to advice

Listen to any advice you are given. Do not dismiss it out of hand. That would be the equivalent of receiving a letter and throwing it away without reading it because you claim that you already know what is in it! Even if you have received similar advice before, sometimes it is the specific way that an individual present's advice that will make it stick this time around.

7. Speak up

Sometimes you have to ask for help, as not everyone will notice when you are struggling. If you find this difficult, try to go to the person you find the most approachable or even take someone with you to help you explain. Sometimes it worth sending an email if you can't handle or initiate a conversation face to face.

8. Work in manageable chunks

There is nothing more soul destroying than setting yourself an unachievable task. Think about times when you have sat through long and intense study sessions, where you have struggled to concentrate, and remember how bad that felt. Set realistic time slots for work and stick to them.

9. Avoid procrastination

It is all too easy to find other things to do when we should be working. It is much harder to focus and concentrate on the job in hand. Try to recognise the difference between having a break and procrastination, which is essentially avoiding getting started. Typically, a break has a time limit and you will know exactly when you stopped work and when you are going to restart. Procrastination is vague and usually only loosely connected to your study, such as tidying your room or desk. Often it is not connected to your study at all, such as making a quick phone call or checking messages.

10. Practise - make use of mark schemes and past papers

There is no substitute for practise. Familiarise yourself with exam requirements. Mark schemes and past papers are available on exam board websites and from teachers. They will help you understand how and why examiners award marks, see the range and scope of questions, and recognise that while the wording of questions changes, the questions are still drawing upon the same blocks of knowledge. In other words, mark schemes and past papers contain information that will help you succeed, so use them.

The students who undertake meaningful practise are much more likely to achieve their potential.

Summary

In order to do all the above to the best of your ability, you need to look after yourself. This means getting some exercise, making sure you get enough sleep, eating well and increasing your water intake. All these things will make sure you are healthy enough to work effectively and retain information.

Adopting a positive and practical approach is the best way to achieve your potential and remember: it's never too late to improve. Even if you have left your revision to the last minute, there is always something you can learn in the remaining time available. It is important to recognise that you don't need to know everything. If time is limited, focus on the essential blocks of knowledge.

Only concern yourself with things you can control. If you have done everything within your control, then you have done as much as you can be expected to do.

Avoid too much comparison with your peers. Listening to what others tell you they have done, or making assumptions about what they have done, is not necessarily accurate or helpful.

75

Aim as high as possible but be realistic. A* is not the only grade. If you achieve a lower result, it still may be enough to get you to the next level. And above all: Never give up!

Part 4: Practical approaches to study

There are many ways in which we can approach learning and the approaches included in this guide are examples of ones that I have seen work with many different students. It is always advisable however to adapt strategies to suit the individual, so in practice I adapt the approach after getting to know each student and identifying which specific methods work best for them as an individual. With that in mind, the following ideas provide models that anyone can use to develop their own unique approaches and strategies for learning.

Helping your teenager get organised

Getting organised early is ideal but even when revision has been left to the last minute, a couple of weeks or days can still help and may be just enough to get a student through an exam and to the next stage. So the message is never give up. Instead of regretting time lost, parents can help their teenager get organised and maximise the time left by supporting them in making a timetable, identifying their most effective learning strategies, emphasising the importance of controlled assessments and coursework and by encouraging exam practice.

Helping your teenager write an effective timetable

The best timetables are specific, detailed and realistic. Many students show me timetables that do not include time to relax or even eat! Poor timetables are also typically characterised by a lack of detail and direction, which in practice is extremely unhelpful. A poor timetable tends to cause more pressure not less, while a well-planned timetable removes a great deal of stress and worry. Countless hours can be wasted by students confused and overwhelmed because they literally do not know what to do next!

Step 1

The first step is to divide the days into workable chunks. I find it is most effective to divide each day into three simple sections: morning, afternoon and evening, then allow each individual student to decide on the times each slot refers to. These times may vary each day depending upon other commitments. For example, if your son or daughter attends a club, has a part-time job or is going to a social event, they may need to adapt the times on that day or indeed on the next day, too. Also, if school is still taking place, then attendance is the priority. It is only during study leave and at weekends that students can be flexible with time. During term time, a timetable may therefore look something like the basic school term timetable below. Note that there will be variations in the times that different year groups are required to be in school.

Basic school term timetable

	Morning	Afternoon	Evening
Sun	10 until 12.30	2 until 4	7 until 9
Mon	School/College	School/College	6 until 8
Tues	School/College	2 until 4 (free lesson)	6 until 8
Weds	School/College	School/College	6 until 8
Thurs	School/College	2 until 4 (free lesson)	6 until 8
Fri	School/College	School/College	5 until 7
Sat	10 until 12	3 until 5	6 until 8

During study leave or holidays, time slots on a timetable may look more like those on the basic study leave timetable below. It is important to note that the time slots I have put into the timetable models are each two hours long and should contain breaks when necessary. Some students will work best in smaller chunks of 30 minutes or an hour. Others will get engrossed and work longer than intended. The most important thing is that your teenager does not make an unachievable timetable, with extensive time slots through which it is impossible to maintain concentration. It is best to keep allocated time slots shorter, then if your teenager comfortable doing more, he or she will have achieved more than planned, not less. Psychologically, this is much more satisfying. And remember, not all of these time slots have to be used!

<u>Basic Study Leave Timetable</u>

	Morning	Afternoon	Evening
Sun	10 to 12	2 to 4	7 to 9
Mon	9 to 11	1 to 3	6 to 8
Tues	9 to 11	1 to 3	6 to 8
Weds	9 to 11	1 to 3	6 to 8
Thurs	10 to 12	1 to 3	6 to 8
Fri	9 to 11	1 to 3	5 to 7
Sat	11 to 1	3 to 5	5 to 7

<u>Step 2</u>

The next step is to put in important events and activities, such as known assessments or exam dates and opportunities for exercise. A timetable should also include social events and while I am aware that for some parents and students this sounds too good to be true, it really is important. Many parents and students feel that social lives should completely stop during the exam months but this isn`t always really realistic. Arguing about whether or not to let a teenager go to a party can waste a lot of time and energy. Sometimes it's more productive to negotiate a reduced social life, and timetable in a few key events that would cause more stress and bad feeling if missed. We must remember though, that ultimately parents are in control and social events are not an automatic inclusion, just a sensible one, as miserable and resentful students do not tend to study well. Obviously social events should only feature if the student has a significant amount of time remaining until exams. I would obviously not advocate going to a party if an exam is imminent and a student is not prepared.

<u>Study leave timetable with key social events</u>

	Morning	Afternoon	Evening
Sun	10 to 12	Family lunch	7 to 9
Mon	Dentist	1 to 3	6 to 8
Tues	9 to 11	1 to 3	6 to 8
Wed	9 to 11	2 to 4	Football
Thur	10 to 12	2 to 4	Run
Fri	9 to 11	1 to 3	Friend's party
Sat	Sleep in	1 to 3	5 to 7

Step 3

The next stage in producing an effective timetable is to decide upon the detail. The student needs to specify exactly what they are going to do in each time slot. When left to their own devices, many students will initially produce a timetable that resembles the one below.

Common student timetable

Sun	History Maths
Mon	History
Tue	History
Wed	Maths
Thur	Maths
Fri	Sociology
Sat	Sociology Maths

Timetables like this rarely work, as even the most organised student benefits from some direction. The danger of skeleton timetables is that the student can waste time deciding or worrying about where to start and how much to do.

To begin filling in a timetable, a student needs a detailed list of what needs to be studied for each subject and the specific detail of what they need to do. For example, for an English Literature GCSE, they may need to do something like this (depending on the specific syllabus and year of entry):

Eng Lit. Paper 1

Of Mice and Men

Sect A

Tasks

1. Re read the text.
2. Make notes on each character (Candy, Crooks, etc.)
3. Make notes on the key themes (American Dream, masculinity, power etc.)
4. Find examples and quotations from the text to support each point
5. Plan whole essays using questions from past papers.
6. Practise writing introductions and topic sentences for each question.
7. Do some actual timed essays.

An Inspector Calls

Sect B

Tasks

1. Re-read the text
2. Make notes on each character and key themes
3. Consider the style and use of questioning
4. Plan whole essays using questions from past papers
5. Practise writing introductions to each question
6. Do some actual timed essays

Eng Lit Paper 2

Sect A

Poetry collection: Relationships

1. Read poems and annotations made in class
2. Consider structure, form, language techniques, themes, messages and voice for each poem.

Sect B

Unseen poems

1. Look for structure, form, language techniques, themes, messages and voice
2. Practise unseen questions

I must stress that this is an example. It is up to the individual student to decide what they actually need to do to prepare for each paper and their school teachers will have given them the exam information they need to make these decisions. The information for each subject can then be inserted into the study timetable in a specific and detailed way, so that each time slot is focused and productive.

Detailed and specific study leave timetable

	Morning	Afternoon	Evening
Sun	10-12 Revision Eng Lit Paper 1 Of Mice and Men Make 4 points on each character. Link to key themes and context. Find supporting evidence/quotation s from the text.	Family lunch	7-9 Spanish Unit1 Listening and Understanding Use BBC Bite size listening activities. Complete a past listening paper.
Mon	9-11 Revision Spanish Unit 1 Listening and Understanding	1.00 pm EXAM Spanish Unit 1 Listening and Understanding	6-8 Revision Eng Lit Paper 1 An Inspector

	Use BBC Bite size listening activities. Complete a past listening paper.		Calls Make 4 points on each character. Link to key themes and context. Find supporting evidence/quotations from the text.
Tues	9.00am EXAM. Eng Lit Paper 1 Exploring modern texts	1-3 Revision Media Revise Moving Image: film language, action/adventure genre. Use past papers.	6-8 Revision Media Revise Lifestyle Mags: genre, layout, representation and stereotypes. Use past papers.
Wed	9.00am EXAM Media Studies Textual Analysis	2-4	Football match
Thur	9-11 Revision History British Depth Study 1850-1918.	2-4	6-8 Revision History British Depth Study 1850-

	Revise context knowledge using flash cards/past papers. Topics: Poverty, Social reform, Liberal Gov, Suffragettes, Women and war effort		1918 Revise context knowledge using flash cards/past papers. Topics: Women and vote, Propaganda, Paris Peace Convention and Germany
Fri	9-11 Revision History Flash cards	1.00pm EXAM History British Depth Study	Friend's party
Sat	Sleep in	1-3	

It might be a good idea to highlight the actual exams and revision sessions in different colours so the student can literally see the exams approaching. That way they will feel more in control. (Please note that I have underlined the exams and revision sessions in the following timetable, in case text is being read in black and white only)

Timetable highlighting exam dates

	Morning	Afternoon	Evening
Sun	10-12 **Revision** Eng Lit Paper 1 Of Mice and Men Make 4 points on each character. Link to key themes and context. Find supporting evidence/quotations from the text.	Family lunch	7-9 **Revision** Spanish Unit 1 Listening and Understanding Use BBC Bite size listening activities. Complete a past listening paper.
Mon	10-12 **Revision** Spanish Unit 1 Listening and Understanding Use BBC Bite size listening activities. Complete a past listening paper.	**1.00pm EXAM Spanish Revision Unit 1 Listening and Understan ding**	6-8 **Revision** Eng Lit Paper 1 An Inspector Calls Make 4 points on each character. Link to key themes and context. Find supporting evidence/quot ations from the text.
Tues	**9.00am EXAM Eng Lit Paper 1 Exploring modern texts.**	1-3 Media **Revision** Moving Image: film language,	6-8 Media **Revision** Lifestyle Mags: Genre, layout, representation

		action/adventure genre. Use past papers.	and stereotypes. Use past papers.
Wed	**9.00am EXAM** **Media Studies Textual Analysis**	2-4	Football match
Thur	9-11 **Revision** History British Depth Study 1850-1918 Revise context knowledge using flash cards/past papers. Poverty, Social reform, Liberal Gov, Suffragettes, Women and war effort.	2-4	6-8 **Revision** History British Depth Study 1850-1918 Revise context knowledge using flash cards/past papers. Women and vote, Propaganda, Paris Peace Convention and Germany.
Fri	9-11 **Revision** History Flash cards	**1.00pm EXAM History British Depth Study**	Friend's party
Sat	Sleep in	1-3	

Be aware of learning approaches and strategies

Individuals learn in many different ways, which can vary across subjects and tasks. It is important, therefore, when preparing for exams to be able and willing to change tactics if a method or approach does not appear to be working. Parents can help their teenager by discussing different approaches to learning and the practical methods involved. In this way parents will be encouraging teenagers to find the most effective ways to study that will help them maximise results.

There are many learning style models in existence, many of which identify and address quite similar features of learning. Some of these frequently occurring features are definitely worth pondering when thinking about an individual's preferred approach. And while an individual may have a preference, it is also quite common for a student to be most productive and learn most effectively when applying different strategies at different stages in the learning process. Just because a student has a preference, it does not mean that adopting other approaches will not be of benefit. If students are given opportunities to attempt and practise different methods of accessing knowledge, they may be surprised by how much they gain.

And remember that learning journeys and revision journeys are different things. You can only revise things you already know, so teenagers may use different strategies to learn, different strategies to revise and different strategies again to consolidate.

Common learning strategies and terms that parents and teenagers may have already come across include some of the approaches listed below. Use this list to work out which strategies may be of benefit. But remember, teenagers should not be labelled as a specific type of learner as most teenagers will benefit from a combination of approaches.

Practical/have a go approach

Practical/have a go approaches include activities which develop learning through real and practical situations. These activities include solving problems and using definite and tangible techniques.

Students get the opportunity to actively embrace new challenges. They can enjoy thinking on their feet and simply having a go. This type of approach is often enjoyed by teenagers who want to be active, rather than passive learners. Having a go can involve being in the spotlight and so these students need to be comfortable working while others watch and learn.

This learning approach is more complicated for students who are worried about failing or who lack self-confidence. However, the approach can be used by individuals who are usually happy to stay in the background, as when revising alone they have the privacy they need in which to make mistakes. An activity that might suit this type of student is to have a go at an exam paper without looking at the mark scheme first. This activity would allow them to create their own baseline, by identifying exactly where they are in terms of their learning and exams skills.

Thinking/reflecting approach

This is an approach where students like to have time to think and take in information at their own pace. They are happy to listen, absorb and reflect. Students who favour this approach like to have the time to investigate ideas and materials. They enjoy observing activities, as they feel they learn from watching and thinking rather than jumping straight in. The type of activities such students might find useful are analysing model answers before attempting a question themselves, reading and taking notes, or watching an educational demonstration on the internet. These students often benefit from being able to visualise and understand something before having a go at it themselves. An example might include a language student who needs to hear a new word spoken before attempting the pronunciation or accent, a science student who needs to see an experiment or a diagram of that experiment before being able to explain it and an English student who needs to analyse the structure of an essay before writing one.

This approach does not work as well for students who are not keen to listen and analyse, or who resist writing things down. Also, students who want to move through activities quickly sometimes find this approach less helpful. Eventually, however, all learning has to be recorded in some way and students will benefit from the experience of committing their learning to paper.

Concluding /theorising approach

This learning approach is often preferred by students who like structures, concepts and theories, and enjoy exploring and questioning such structures and theories. These students tend to have a logical approach to learning and feel secure when there is a clear context. They also like to apply theory and identify its relevance. An example might be a student studying a poem being given a basic concept (such as the poem exploring aspects of sibling rivalry) then being allowed to work out the rest for themselves. In terms of science, a student might be given a theory and then a scenario in which to investigate it, with a view to either supporting or challenging the theory.

This learning approach does not tend to be enjoyed as much, at least initially, by students who are not comfortable asking questions or who are nervous about being stretched outside their comfort zone. It is not always favoured by students who prefer to be more spontaneous and intuitive in their approach to learning.

Visual strategies

Some students feel that they learn best when they can visualise ideas. They may, for example, like to organise their revision using diagrams, maps, colours, layouts that utilise whitespace, charts and so on, in order to make clear connections between ideas.

Auditory strategies

Auditory strategies work with students who enjoy listening, discussing ideas and using spoken language (such as stating questions and answers in their own words). These students may need a parent to test them, listen while they explain ideas, or simply have a discussion with them. It is not necessary for a parent to be an authority on any subject. The student will simply benefit from their parent acting as a sounding board. Providing your teenager with an opportunity to explain will allow them to consolidate their understanding. Questions will be generated and their knowledge will develop as they search for answers.

Kinesthetic strategies

This approach is about learning through action and movement, through real and relevant activities. Students may enjoy the physical aspect as they prefer moving to sitting still. These students may dislike a lecture-style lesson, for example, and often benefit from working in short bursts. Some concentrate better if making movements while learning, such as squeezing a stress ball or tapping a pencil. Others work particularly well with flash cards as they enjoy the game element. These students often need lots of examples to illustrate and consolidate their learning.

Mix and match approaches

The interesting thing about strategies for learning, such as those outlined above, and the preferences that an individual student may adopt, is that these practices can be cross referenced. In other words, they can be used and applied to a task in any order a student sees fit. In this way, students can personalise the way they learn and revise, which is another reason why it is important to encourage children to take ownership of their education. It is much more likely they will develop learning techniques that work for them if they have a real interest in the outcome.

Even though students will have aspects of learning that they enjoy more than others, it is still good practice to adopt some kind of balance. For example, if a student prefers a theorising or concluding approach to learning, they may benefit from trying a more thinking/reflective approach because the tendency to jump to conclusions without thinking things through or testing possibilities may potentially limit learning. In the same way, a student who simply thinks and reflects might be in danger of never fully reaching a conclusion, so it is important to balance this approach with a theorising/concluding approach.

Teachers will try to give a balance and variety of learning strategies in their teaching and also to change the order of approaches to learning when presenting information. It is good practice to do this. Parents need to recognise that it is also good practice to help their children identify the best approaches for them. It is equally important for parents to recognise that their children may learn in ways that are different to the way they learn, so it is important to avoid jumping to conclusions about learning strategies. For example, I have come across many students who tap their pens or rock backwards and forwards on their chairs while learning. To some, this might appear to be a sign that they are not concentrating. However, it has proved to be a comfortable way for them to learn. There are also students who will frequently get up from their place of study or simply need to move around while working. Again, to some this might seem like an unnecessary distraction, but many students simply need to move and have a break when absorbing a new idea.

Procrastination or work avoidance, however, are completely different issues. Parents need to use their knowledge of their children and their habits, to read the situation. For example, the continual leaving of a work area may be an indication that a student is avoiding revision, is simply not motivated, or does not know where to begin. These are very different problems and ones that must be addressed by the parent and in partnership with teachers through discussion and practical support when needed.

Part 5: Looking ahead

Results day

You and your teenager have got through the pressure of exams and it's finally time to get the results of all that hard work. Again, remember that this day is all about the student, so no matter how you as a parent may feel about your teenager's results, what matters is how your teenager feels about them.

It is also a good idea to avoid comparing your teenager's results to others as another student's success or underachievement has no impact upon your child. Also, from a sensitivity perspective, it is probably best to avoid asking other teenagers about their grades as you will not know how they truly feel about their results and could risk upsetting them.

Hopefully, if all has gone according to plan, everyone will be celebrating. If that is not the case, however, parents should continue to practise and demonstrate positive thinking techniques and ensure that they do not accidentally communicate disappointment to their teenager in an unhelpful way. It is perfectly natural to feel disappointed on behalf of a teenager who is feeling disappointed themselves but parents still need to remember that what is said now really matters in terms of helping their teenager to keep a positive outlook so that they can continue to pursue future success. Keeping a realistic yet positive perspective and continuing to support your teenager through to the next level is something that your teenager will always remember and appreciate in the years to come.

A Bright Future

I would like to end this guide with a case study that emphasises the extent to which a positive approach from parents can really alleviate stress for their teenager. Such on-going positive and realistic support helps a teenager cope when they experience disappointment and helps them take steps towards securing a brighter future.

Case Study: Lola, a Y12 student

Lola spent Y11 working extremely hard to achieve the grade B in English Language needed to enter her chosen sixth form. Lola worried about her work and was prone to feeling overwhelmed at times. Her mum was consistently supportive, positive and realistic which meant that Lola always seemed to be able to pick herself up and carry on when she encountered a minor set-back. Her mum was key to this as she frequently reinforced and modelled an optimistic perspective, explaining to Lola that there were many routes through life whilst always encouraging her to do her best. Lola's mum communicated to Lola that she was proud of her and her work ethic no matter what result she received. On results day Lola had to face a bigger hurdle. She found out that she had received a C in English Language and was now unable to begin her chosen courses at her chosen school. Lola was extremely disappointed and tearful as she now had to rethink her next steps.

I saw Lola and her mum two weeks after she received her results and was over the moon to find them both smiling. Lola told me that although she had felt very sad on results day and for a few days after, she had then spent her time investigating other options. She found that she was interested in a BTEC Level 3 course which was on offer at a local college. She immediately applied and was offered a place. Lola explained that although this was not a direction she had ever imagined herself taking, she was now extremely excited. She went so far as to say that in a way she was glad that she hadn't achieved the B as she may never had found or considered this course. Lola also had found out that she could go to University from a BTEC level 3 course in the same way that she could from A Levels, something of which she had not been aware.

This case study really is testament to the power of positive, supportive parents. Throughout Year 11,

Lola's mum had consistently communicated that Lola was more important than the exams and shown her that there were many ways of achieving her potential. She had used her knowledge of Lola to spot the warning signs and to intercept when she could see stress levels increasing. She had helped Lola develop a positive outlook and a realistic perspective. As a result Lola was able to deal with disappointment and set back. She was able to actively seek out another route and make her own future bright and positive.

Positive attitudes, realistic perspectives and a willingness to let teenagers progress and develop at their own pace will most certainly reduce stress levels during the exam months. When parents encourage teenagers to be independent and take ownership of their own lives they really are helping them to fulfil their potential and this positive and practical approach to study is not only a gift worth giving, but an invaluable present for any young person to receive.

Testimonials

'My son is not a conventional learner, and although he is bright, finds it hard to focus and get essays written. Bernie Jones provided on-going support for him throughout his GCSE's and A levels and her calm approach helped me keep perspective too. It is easy for parents to get stressed out, which has a negative affect all round. Bernie's method of positive support and encouragement gives great results and builds confidence in her students. Her approach focuses on the individual and enables them to make self-assured choices.'

Jane (parent)

My son had totally lost his way half way through his first year of A levels and was struggling to keep on track with his course – Bernie's calm, friendly, fun approach was just what he needed to boost his morale so he believed in himself again and had the confidence not only to continue the course but to actually enjoy it. By the end of the process he was noticeably a changed person with renewed enthusiasm and confidence and went on to pass!

Debbie (parent)

'I was very complacent whilst in my lessons as I was not enjoying learning about the subjects that I was studying, a large part of Y12 was spent questioning whether or not to drop out of sixth form altogether as I felt A levels were a step too far for me and I wasn't confident I'd even pass one of my subjects. I often regard Bernie as the main reason I passed my A levels and eventually got into my first choice University. Not just was Bernie exceptional at putting the content into a way that I would understand but she most importantly changed my whole mind-set towards my work.

I would often feel overwhelmed by the coursework/revision I had been set for that week and Bernie made me see that it was of course doable and in fact not as hard as I thought. This was mainly down to her calm and encouraging nature and her ability to make every task seem as if it was nothing to panic about.

As great as Bernie is at teaching I felt that the reason she helped me the most was because of how great she was to talk to. Always chilled out despite how last-minute I was with seeking help with all my work. Always encouraging and able to find the good in my work despite me often thinking it wasn't even worth a read; but also very funny and a teacher who I can easily admit I used to enjoy going to!'

Todd (Uni student)

Bernie Jones has supported my two sons in their English exams. They had very different concerns and she really listened to them and helped them feel confident and positive about their knowledge and ability. She reduced their fear of the exam process by increasing their understanding of the papers and by helping them see that they already had many of the tools they needed. She did not compare them, instead she focused on helping them work to their strengths. In the wider scheme Bernie Jones encouraged both them and me to see that they were worth so much more than the marks they achieved and that each would be able to pursue their goals. Her understanding of the different routes to success was inspiring and reassuring.

Phaedra (parent)

Bernie was always prepared for lessons and she really knew what she was doing. I always felt that she wanted me to do well. She was chilled but made it clear what I had to do each week. It was really helpful to go through essays because Bernie made me understand what the examiners would be looking for in the real thing.

Yonina (Y11 Student)

Bernie helped two of my daughters with their GSCE English – and both received A* in their exams. Bernie is very focussed and constructive in her comments, while at the same time being a friendly and encouraging teacher. I was confident that Bernie's extensive experience as a classroom teacher meant that she understood exactly the sort of assistance my daughters needed.

Sally (parent)

Our son was struggling in his English GCSE class and her positive support and encouragement gave him back his confidence and enjoyment of this subject. Her relaxed approach and sense of humour were a welcome relief from the pressure during the exam months. He then went on to study for a BTEC in digital film production, which he has a great interest in, and this led to him gaining a place at University to study for a BA (Hons) in Film-making. Bernie's general ethos that there is more than one pathway to University plus her continued support were invaluable throughout this stressful time.

Karen (parent)

22552444R00065

Printed in Poland
by Amazon Fulfillment
Poland Sp. z o.o., Wrocław